£5.50

D1580148

A Calendar of Poems

Poems collected by Wes Magee

Bell & Hyman

Published in 1986 by
BELL & HYMAN LIMITED
Denmark House
37-39 Queen Elizabeth Street
London SE1 2QB

This selection © Wes Magee 1986
Copyright of individual poems as listed in
Acknowledgements section
Illustrations © Bell & Hyman Limited

British Library Cataloguing in Publication Data

A calendar of poems
  1. English poetry
  I. Magee, Wes
  821'.008'09282   PR1175

  ISBN 0-7135-2590-8

Designed by Andrew Shoolbred
Cover and text illustrations by Gary Wing

Printed in Great Britain by
The Bath Press, Avon

Contents

Contents

Contents

Contents

Contents

The year

JANUARY falls the snow,
FEBRUARY cold winds blow,
In MARCH peep out the early flowers,
And APRIL comes with sunny showers.
In MAY the roses bloom so gay,
In JUNE the farmer mows his hay,
In JULY brightly shines the sun,
In AUGUST harvest is begun.
SEPTEMBER turns the green leaves brown,
OCTOBER winds then shake them down,
NOVEMBER fills with blear and smear,
DECEMBER comes and ends the year.

FLORA WATSON

January

New Year morning — just after midnight

Oh dear, oh dear, I have not since last year
Had a wash,
Combed my hair,
Cleaned my teeth,
Worn my clothes,
Got out of bed,
Been to sleep,
Opened the curtains,
Had a meal,
Done any work,
Fed the chickens,
Lit a fire,
Baked a cake,
Spent a coin,
Earned a penny,
Done a good deed,
Said a prayer,
Had a letter,
Used the 'phone . . . How did the time just disappear?
I'll try to make up things, don't fear,
But,
I've done nothing since last year.

GREGORY HARRISON

Winter days

Biting air
Winds blow
City streets
Under snow

Noses red
Lips sore
Runny eyes
Hands raw

Chimneys smoke
Cars crawl
Piled snow
On garden wall

Slush in gutters
Ice in lanes
Frosty patterns
On window panes

Morning call
Lift up head
Nipped by winter
Stay in bed

GARETH OWEN

Snow and ice poems

(i)

Our street is dead lazy
especially in winter.
Some mornings you wake up
and it's still lying there
saying nothing. Huddled
under its white counterpane.

But soon the lorries arrive
like angry mums,
pull back the blankets
and send it shivering
off to work.

(ii)

Winter
morning.
Snowflakes
for breakfast.
The street
outside
quiet
as a
long
white
bandage.

ROGER McGOUGH

First snow

Whose is this long, unexpected elbow
Resting its white sleeve on the wall?
Is anyone out there when I call
To hear my voice? I've lost my echo.

Whose are these feathery tears that keep coming?
Somebody weeps without a sound
And leaves his grief heaped up on the ground.
It's so quiet my ears are drumming.

Whose is that handkerchief on the gatepost
Large enough for a giant sneeze?
Bless you whisper the shivering trees
While I just stand here like a ghost.

Who am I? And where have I woken?
It wasn't the same when I went to bed.
I still feel me inside my head
Though now a different language is spoken.

Suddenly all the meanings have gone.
Is someone trying to tell me something?
A bird shakes silver dust from its wing
And the sky goes on and on and on.

JOHN MOLE

The frozen man

Out at the edge of town
where black trees

crack their fingers
in the icy wind

and hedges freeze
on their shadows

and the breath of cattle,
still as boulders,

hangs in rags
under the rolling moon,

a man is walking
alone:

on the coal-black road
his cold

feet
ring

and
ring.

Here in a snug house
at the heart of town

the fire is burning
red and yellow and gold:

you can hear the warmth
like a sleeping cat

breathe softly
in every room.

When the frozen man
comes to the door,

let him in,
let him in,
let him in.

KIT WRIGHT

From the winter wind
a cold fly
came to our window
where we had frozen our noses
and warmed his feet on the glass

MICHAEL ROSEN

Black clouds

Into the playground we went,
Stephen, Rick and I,
And I looked up into the hazy sky.
Black clouds in the distance,
Black clouds overhead,
'It's cold out here,' I shivered,
'It's cold out here,' I said.

Stephen he stood standing there,
The wind it curled his dark brown hair.
'Come on, I'll race you, Tom,' he said,
So round the playground once we sped.
Black clouds in the distance,
Black clouds overhead,
'It's cold out here,' I shivered,
'It's cold out here,' I said.

TERENCE BRAME

A skiing song for January

A silver sky is faintly etched;
White against white the world is stretched;
The silence beats through a distant hum,
And down the slopes the skiers come.

Then it's hi! ho! hi!
When the woods all lie
A-huddling close toward a wintry sky.
And it's ho! hi! ho!
When the white winds blow,
And the whole world sweeps
Down the steeps
Of the snow.

MICHAEL LEWIS

January moon

The moon skates through the sky
Against the wind, against
The low-flying clouds.
On blue ice she dances
Soundlessly.

GERDA MAYER

In the garden in winter

In the garden in winter
One rose
Like a creamy ice cream cornet
Still grows.

In the garden in winter
Two pears
That ripened all summer
Still hang there.

In the garden in winter
Three birds
Peck each other
And the bread.

In the garden in winter
Four trees
With leafless boughs
Comb the breeze.

In the garden in winter
Five cabbages grow
And wait to be eaten
In a row.

In the garden in winter
Six steps of stone
Are the only things
That don't feel cold.

In the garden in winter
Seven days of the week
Beneath the ground
The flower bulbs sleep.

STANLEY COOK

February

The snowdrop

Many, many welcomes,
February fair-maid,
Ever as of old time,
Solitary firstling,
Coming in the cold time.
Many, many welcomes,
February fair-maid!

ALFRED, LORD TENNYSON

Sheep in winter

The sheep get up and make their many tracks
And bear a load of snow upon their backs,
And gnaw the frozen turnip to the ground
With sharp quick bite, and then go noising round
The boy that pecks the turnips all the day
And knocks his hands to keep the cold away
And laps his legs in straw to keep them warm
And hides behind the hedges from the storm.
The sheep, as tame as dogs, go where he goes
And try to shake their fleeces from the snows,
Then leave their frozen meal and wander round
The stubble stack that stands beside the ground,
And lie all night and face the drizzling storm
And shun the hovel where they might be warm.

JOHN CLARE

February

Around, above the world of snow
The light-heeled breezes breathe and blow;
Now here, now there, they wheel the flakes,
And whistle through the sun-dried brakes,
Then, growing faint, in silence fall
Against the keyhole in the hall.

Then dusky twilight spreads around,
The last soft snowflake seeks the ground,
And through unshaded window panes
The lamp-rays strike across the plains,
While now and then a shadow tall
Is thrown upon the whitewashed wall.

The hoar frost crackles on the trees,
The rattling brook begins to freeze,
The well sweep glistens in the light
As if with dust of diamonds bright;
And spreading over the crusted snow
A few swift-footed rabbits go.

Then the night silence, long and deep,
When weary eyes close fast in sleep;
The hush of Nature's breath, until
The cock crows loud upon the hill;
And shortly through the eastern haze
The red sun sets the sky ablaze.

JAMES BENSEL

Shrove Tuesday rhyme

Snick, snock, the pan's hot,
Here we come a-shroving.
Please to give us something,
Something's better than nothing!
A bit of bread, a bit of cheese,
A bit of apple dumpling, please!

ANON.

The pancake

Mix a pancake,
Stir a pancake,
    Pop it in the pan.
Fry the pancake,
Toss the pancake,
    Catch it if you can.

CHRISTINA ROSSETTI

Frost

A busy sprite, Frost,
    For sparkling and clean
Are meadowlands where
    His white feet have been.

The grey wintry grasses,
    So soiled and so dim,
Wear fringes of silver
    All fashioned by him.

The wheel-ruts and hollows
    Are muddy no more,
But crisp to my footsteps —
    A diamonded floor.

And windows are studded
    With drawings like dreams,
Of fragile white forests,
    And towers, and streams.

L. M. DUFTY

Winter birds

Most mornings now they're there,
Humped on the chestnut fence
Awaiting the regular hour
That brings me out of the shower,
Warm, pulling on my pants,
Enjoying a last yawn.
They might have been there since dawn,

And have been for all I know.
So I crumble up their bread
As a famished one or two
Hop down on to the snow —
Thrushes, all bold eye
And cream and coffee feather.
How they confront the weather!

It is habit, I suppose,
That brings these birds to wait,
And the natures that they all
So variously inherit
Show up as they strut and eat —
These starlings now, they call
Their friends to share the meal.

And when all seems to have gone
An elegant wagtail comes,
Turning his slender neck
And precise, selective beak
To feed on specks so small
They seem not there at all.
He eats the crumbs of crumbs.

But the harsh, predatory,
Scavenging, black-headed gulls
Uncertainly wheel and call,
Or balefully sit in the field.

26

Though fiercely hunger pulls
They will not come for the bread
And fly at the lift of my head.

But it is the gulls I hear
As I take the car down the road,
Their voices cold as winter,
Their wings grey as a cloud.
They've had nothing from my hands,
And I wish before dark fall
Some comfort for us all.

LESLIE NORRIS

Robin

If on a frosty morning
the robin redbreast calls
his waistcoat red and burning
like a beggar at your walls

throw bread crumbs on the grass for him
when the ground is hard and still
for in his breast there is a flame
that winter cannot kill.

IAIN CRICHTON SMITH

After breakfast

I stop myself sliding a morsel
Of bacon fat into the bin.
It will do as a meal for the robin,
His legs are so terribly thin.

ROY FULLER

Giant Winter

Giant Winter preys on the earth,
Gripping with talons of ice,
Squeezing, seeking a submission,
Tightening his grip like a vice.

Starved of sunlight shivering trees
Are bent by his torturing breath.
The seeds burrow into the soil
Preparing to fight to the death.

Giant Winter sneers at their struggles,
Blows blizzards from his frozen jaws,
Ripples cold muscles of iron,
Clenches tighter his icicle claws.

Just as he seems to be winning,
Strength suddenly ebbs from his veins.
He releases his hold and collapses.
Giant Spring gently takes up the reins.

Snarling, bitter with resentment,
Winter crawls to his polar den,
Where he watches and waits till it's time
To renew the battle again.

DEREK STUART

March

It's spring, it's spring

It's spring, it's spring —

when everyone sits round a roaring fire
telling ghost stories!

It's spring, it's spring —

when everyone sneaks into everyone else's yard
and bashes up their snowman!

It's spring, it's spring —

when the last dead leaves fall from the trees
and Granny falls off your toboggan!

It's spring, it's spring —

when you'd give your right arm
for a steaming hot bowl of soup!

It's spring, it's spring —

when you'd give your right leg
not to be made to wash up after Christmas dinner!

It's spring, it's spring —

isn't it?

KIT WRIGHT

Three days into March

Today
the birds sang
and yellow crocuses
opened wide their mouths
to feast on
sunlight.

Today
the sky cleared
and enthusiastic trees
stretched out their limbs
all thick with
promises.

Today
I stood still
and the greens, the blues
and the yellows clamoured
to dance behind
my eyes.

MOIRA ANDREW

Just a passing shower

sunshine	sunshine	sunshine
sunshine	sunshine	/////
sunshine	/////	sunshine
/////	sunshine	sunshine
sunshine	sunshine	sunshine

ALAN RIDDELL

shower

fierce
    spring
        rain
           full
               gushing
                 drain
                   grey
drab   puddled
  steely   street
    sky   Wellies
        umbrellas   for
         held   feet
           high
             children
cars   want
  make   out
    spray   harassed
      birds   mothers
        huddle   shout
          away
           cats
rain   lie
  becomes   asleep
    drops   plants
      slows   drink
        and   deep
          stops
         doors
           open
             wide
               people
                 step
                   outside

MOIRA ANDREW

Calendar of cloud

A springtime cloud is
    sudden grief
    a sneak-thief
squeezing the morning dry.

A summer cloud is
    a wishbone
    a fishbone
filletted clean from sky.

An autumn cloud is
    a broomstick
    a doomstick
chasing cobwebs into night.

A winter cloud is
    a bucketful
    a ducking-stool
dowsing every thing in sight.

MOIRA ANDREW

First day of spring

First day of spring,
a girl and two boys
are mending a puncture.

The weak sun spikes the water
in the basin
and the bubbles from
the submerged inner tube
rise up like tiny, transparent balls.

Spanners, oil can, repair kit,
spoons and screwdrivers all lie
on the pavement warming their winter metal.

A girl and two boys
are mending a puncture
under a thin cloud
beside nodding daffodils
a new bike for a new yellow year.

JOHN RICE

In March

The snow melts
exposing what was
buried there all winter —
tricycles and
fire-engines and
all sizes of children
waiting in boots and
yellow mackintoshes
for the mud.

ANNE STEVENSON

The river in March

Now the river is rich, but her voice is low.
It is her Mighty Majesty the sea
Travelling among the villages incognito.

Now the river is poor. No song, just a thin mad whisper.
The winter floods have ruined her.
She squats between draggled banks, fingering her rags and rubbish.

And now the river is rich. A deep choir.
It is the lofty clouds, that work in heaven,
Going on their holiday to the sea.

The river is poor again. All her bones are showing.
Through a dry wig of bleached flotsam she peers up ashamed
From her slum of sticks.

Now the river is rich, collecting shawls and minerals.
Rain brought fatness, but she takes ninety-nine percent
Leaving the fields just one percent to survive on.

And now she is poor. Now she is East wind sick.
She huddles in holes and corners. The brassy sun gives her a headache.
She has lost all her fish. And she shivers.

But now once more she is rich. She is viewing her lands.
A hoard of king-cups spills from her folds, it blazes, it cannot be hidden.
A salmon, a sow of solid silver,

Bulges to glimpse it.

TED HUGHES

April

Firefox

Fox fox
coat of fire
bush of flame
setting light
to April woods
firework trail
of powder, fuse
that sets aglow
with green and gold
the willow wands
the meadow grass
the pasture ponds
the primrose banks.

Fox fox fox
from winter runs
with torch for tail
and touches spring
to hill and copse
his foxfire fingers
flaming hedges
spreading shoots of
shivering blossom
in the sun – – the ghost
of summertime
that trots beside
his crimson shadow's
violet and bluebell glades – –

mysterious barks – fox, fox,
fox, fox – fox, fox, fox – fox – fox!

JAMES KIRKUP

Now the sleeping creatures waken —
      Waken, waken;
Blossoms with soft winds are shaken —
      Shaken, shaken;
Squirrels scamper and the hare
Runs races which the children share
Till their shouting fills the air.

Now the woodland birds are singing —
      Singing, singing;
Over field and orchard winging —
      Winging, winging;
Swift and swallow unaware
Weave such beauty on the air
That the children hush and stare.

RAYMOND WILSON

The nest

Don't move —
　　don't touch —
don't speak —
　　do you see
a blackbird's nest
　　in the holly tree?

Look very carefully
　　in between
last year's prickle
　　and this year's green . . .

Timid and brown
　　the mother bird
listens, and watches.
　　Has she heard?

Whisper —
　　whisper —
do you see
　　a blackbird's nest
in the holly tree?

JEAN KENWARD

From Home thoughts, from abroad

Oh, to be in England
Now that April's there,
And whoever wakes in England
Sees, some morning, unaware,
That the lowest boughs and the brushwood sheaf
Round the elm-tree bole are in tiny leaf,
While the chaffinch sings on the orchard bough,
In England — now!

ROBERT BROWNING

From Under Milk Wood

There's the clip clop of horses on the sunhoneyed
cobbles of the humming streets, hammering of
horseshoes, gobble quack and cackle, tomtit
twitter from the bird-ounced boughs, braying on
Donkey Down. Bread is baking, pigs are grunting,
chop goes the butcher, milk-churns bell, tills ring,
sheep cough, dogs shout, saws sing. Oh, the Spring
whinny and morning moo from the clog dancing
farms, the gulls' gab and rabble on the boat-bobbing
river and sea and the cockles bubbling in the sand,
scamper of sanderlings, curlew cry, crow caw, pigeon
coo, clock strike, bull bellow, and the ragged gabble
of the beargarden school as the women scratch and
babble in Mrs. Organ Morgan's general shop where
everything is sold: custard, buckets, henna,
rat-traps, shrimp-nets, sugar, stamps, confetti,
paraffin, hatchets, whistles.

DYLAN THOMAS

Sowing beans

One for the mouse,
One for the crow,
One to rot,
One to grow.

ANON.

Sowing

It was a perfect day
For sowing; just
As sweet and dry was the ground
As tobacco-dust.

I tasted deep the hour
Between the far
Owl's chuckling first soft cry
And the first star.

A long stretched hour it was;
Nothing undone
Remained; the early seeds
All safely sown.

And now, hark at the rain,
Windless and light,
Half a kiss, half a tear,
Saying good-night.

EDWARD THOMAS

Springburst

(to be read from the bottom)

FLOWER!
the
slowly   slowly
the petal curling
the bud,
awakening.
Oh, the
up!
straight
I know!
Now
hm.
hm

see.   see.
me   Hm   me
Let   Let
higher . . .
must reach
for the sky —
Now, must reach
I be!
I live!
up
tip
warmth
coolness
water,
food and
life growing,
life, being,
in the dark —
(seed style)
spark
A

JOHN TRAVERS MOORE

Loveliest of trees

Loveliest of trees, the cherry now
Is hung with bloom along the bough,
And stands about the woodland ride
Wearing white for Eastertide.

Now, of my threescore years and ten,
Twenty will not come again,
And take from seventy springs a score,
It only leaves me fifty more.

And since to look at things in bloom
Fifty springs are little room,
About the woodlands I will go
To see the cherry hung with snow.

A. E. HOUSMAN

Father and I in the woods

'Son,'
My father used to say,
'Don't run.'

'Walk,'
My father used to say,
'Don't talk.'

'Words,'
My father used to say,
'Scare birds.'

So be:
It's sky and brook and bird
And tree.

DAVID McCORD

May

May poem

rain falls

the candy-floss tree
rains confetti and
bridesmaids

pink snowdrifts
lie on the path

GERDA MAYER

The trees

The trees are coming into leaf
Like something almost being said;
The recent buds relax and spread,
Their greenness is a kind of grief.

Is it that they are born again
And we grow old? No, they die too.
Their yearly trick of looking new
Is written down in rings of grain.

Yet still the unresting castles thresh
In fullgrown thickness every May.
Last year is dead, they seem to say,
Begin afresh, afresh, afresh.

PHILIP LARKIN

Things to remember

The buttercups in May,
The wild rose on the spray,
The poppy in the hay,

The primrose in the dell,
The freckled foxglove bell,
The honeysuckle's smell

Are things I would remember
When cheerless, raw November
Makes room for dark December.

JAMES REEVES

May

The quick blade's scream
across the orchard; gleam
of naked poplar, elm;
soft sawdust piled at dusk.

JOHN LOVEDAY

Swifts

Fifteenth of May. Cherry blossom. The swifts
Materialise at the tip of a long scream
Of needle. 'Look! They're back! Look!' And they're gone
On a steep

Controlled scream of skid
Round the house-end and away under the cherries. Gone.
Suddenly flickering in sky summit, three or four together,
Gnat-whisp frail, and hover-searching, and listening

For air-chills — are they too early? With a bowing
Power-thrust to left, then to right, then a flicker they
Tilt into a slide, a tremble for balance,
Then lashing down disappearance

Behind elms.

        They've made it again,
Which means the globe's still working, the Creation's
Still waking refreshed, our summer's
Still all to come —

        And here they are, here they are again
Erupting across yard stones
Shrapnel-scatter terror. Frog-gapers,
Speedway goggles, international mobsters —

A bolas of three or four wire screams
Jockeying across each other
On their switchback wheel of death.
They swat past, hard-fletched,

Veer to the hard air, toss up over the roof,
And are gone again. Their mole-dark labouring,
Their lunatic limber scramming frenzy
And their whirling blades
Sparkle out into blue —

50

Not ours any more.
Rats ransacked their nests so now they shun us.
Round luckier houses now
They crowd their evening dirt-track meetings,

Racing their discords, screaming as if speed-burned,
Head-height, clipping the doorway
With their leaden velocity and their butterfly lightness,
Their too much power, their arrow-thwack into the eaves.

Every year a first-fling, nearly-flying
Misfit flopped in our yard,
Groggily somersaulting to get airborne.
He bat-crawled on his tiny useless feet, tangling his flails

Like a broken toy, and shrieking thinly
Till I tossed him up — then suddenly he flowed away under
His bowed shoulders of enormous swimming power,
Slid away along levels wobbling

On the fine wire they have reduced life to,
And crashed among the raspberries.
Then followed fiery hospital hours
In a kitchen. The moustached goblin savage

Nested in a scarf. The bright blank
Blind, like an angel, to my meat-crumbs and flies.
Then eyelids resting. Wasted clingers curled.
The inevitable balsa death.

Finally burial
For the husk
Of my little Apollo —

The charred scream
Folded in its huge power.

TED HUGHES

Earth-worm

Do
you
squirm
when
you
see
an earth-worm?
I never
do squirm
because I think
a big fat worm
is really rather clever
the way it can shrink
and go
so small
without
a sound
into the ground.
And then
what about
all
that
work it does
and no oxygen
or miner's hat?
Marvellous
you have to admit,
even if you don't like fat
pink worms a bit,
how with that
thin
slippery skin
it makes its way
day after day
through the soil,
such honest toil.
And don't forget
the dirt
it eats, I bet
you wouldn't like to come out
at night to squirt
it all over the place
with no eyes in your face:
I doubt
too if you know
an earth-worm is deaf, but
it can hear YOU go
to and fro
even if you cut
it in half.
So
do not laugh
or squirm
again
when
you
suddenly
see
a worm.

LEONARD CLARK

Weathers

This is the weather the cuckoo likes,
    And so do I;
When showers betumble the chestnut spikes,
    And nestlings fly:
And the little brown nightingale bills his best,
And they sit outside at *The Traveller's Rest*,
And girls come forth sprig-muslin dressed,
And citizens dream of the south and west,
    And so do I.

This is the weather the shepherd shuns,
    And so do I;
When beeches drip in browns and duns,
    And thresh, and ply;
And hill-hid tides throb, throe on throe,
And meadow rivulets overflow,
And drops on gate-bars hang in a row,
And rooks in families homeward go,
    And so do I.

THOMAS HARDY

Bluebells

This year and every year
The long-legged trees
Stand, now Spring is here,
In a bright blue sea.

No one can count the bluebells
That gather together
Until they fill
The woods with waves of their colour.

Beneath new shining leaves
On the long-legged trees
Children gathering flowers
Paddle in a bluebell sea.

STANLEY COOK

June

comes

nes summer,
mes summer,
Chirping robin, budding rose.
Here comes summer,
Here comes summer,
Gentle showers, summer clothes.
Here comes summer,
Here comes summer —
Whooosh — shiver — there it goes.

SHEL SILVERSTEIN

Cuckoo song

Summer is icumen in,
Loude sing, cuckoo!

ANON.

The cuckoo

Cuckoo, Cuckoo
What do you do?

In April
I open my bill.

In May
I sing night and day.

In June
I change my tune.

In July
Away I fly.

In August
Go I must.

ANON.

My mother saw a dancing bear

My mother saw a dancing bear
By the schoolyard, a day in June.
The keeper stood with chain and bar
And whistle-pipe, and played a tune.

And Bruin lifted up its head
And lifted up its dusty feet,
And all the children laughed to see
It caper in the summer heat.

They watched as for the Queen it died.
They watched it march. They watched it halt.
They heard the keeper as he cried,
'Now, roly-poly! Somersault!'

And then, my mother said, there came
The keeper with a begging-cup,
The bear with burning coat of fire,
Shaming the laughter to a stop.

They paid a penny for the dance,
But what they saw was not the show;
Only, in Bruin's aching eyes,
Far-distant forests, and the snow.

CHARLES CAUSLEY

Summer shower

Window window window pane:
Let it let it let it rain
Drop by drop by drop by drop.

Run your rivers from the top
Zigzaggy down, like slow wet forks
Of lightning, so the slippery corks
Of bubbles float and overtake
Each other till three bubbles make
A kind of boat too fat to fit
The river. That's the end of it.

> Straight
> down
> it
> slides
> and
> with
> a
> splash

Is lost against the window sash.

Window window window pane:
Let it let it let it rain

DAVID McCORD

Rain

There are holes in the sky
    Where the rain gets in.
But they're ever so small
    That's why rain is thin.

SPIKE MILLIGAN

Adlestrop

Yes, I remember Adlestrop —
The name, because one afternoon
Of heat the express-train drew up there
Unwontedly. It was late June.

The steam hissed. Someone cleared his throat.
No one left and no one came
On the bare platform. What I saw
Was Adlestrop — only the name

And willows, willow-herb, and grass,
And meadowsweet, and haycocks dry,
No whit less still and lonely fair
Than the high cloudlets in the sky.

And for that minute a blackbird sang
Close by, and round him, mistier,
Farther and farther, all the birds
Of Oxfordshire and Gloucestershire.

EDWARD THOMAS

Cut grass

Cut grass lies frail:
Brief is the breath
Mown stalks exhale.
Long, long the death

It dies in the white hours
Of young-leafed June
With chestnut flowers,
With hedges snowlike strewn,

White lilac bowed,
Lost lanes of Queen Anne's lace,
And that high-builded cloud
Moving at summer's pace.

PHILIP LARKIN

The vegetable garden and the runaway horse

In everybody's garden now,
The grass has started growing,
Gardeners, they are gardening,
And mowers . . . they are mowing,
Compost heaps are rotting down,
And bonfires burning low,
So I took up me shovel,
And resolved to have a go.

I dug a patch of garden,
That was not too hot or shady,
And not too large to tax
The constitution of a lady,
Everything which crossed my spade,
I flung it all asunder,
And that which I could not dig up,
I rapidly dug under.

And in my little plot,
I bravely laboured with the hoe,
Enthusiasm running rife,
I sprinted too and fro,
I stopped for nothing,
Not for food or drink or idle words,
Except a spotted dick,
Someone had chucked out for the birds.

Imagine then my pleasure,
As it all came sprouting out,
I cast aside my dibber,
And I swaggered round about,
But, Alas, the gate,
To which my garden was adjacent,
Was open, and I never saw,
As up the path I hastened.

When I went down on Saturday,
A horse stood in my plot,
But nothing else stood in it,
For he'd eaten all the lot,
I said, 'Alas, my efforts wasted,
And my garden wrecked,
Go away, you rotten horse,'
(Or ,words to that effect.)

His hooves had crushed me lettuce,
And me radishes were mangled,
Broken canes were scattered,
Where me runner beans had dangled,
The lovely shiny marrow,
I'd been going to stuff and all,
The horse had broke it off its stalk,
And kicked it up the wall.

Standing in the ruins,
Of me brussels sprouts and spinach,
I threw aside me shovel,
And I said, 'Well, that's the finish,
No more early peas for me,
The birds can have them,
Or the mice might,
And if I want a cabbage,
Well, I'll see you down at Pricerite!'

PAM AYRES

LARK
spi
nni
ng
at
the
pe
ak
of
an
inv
isi
ble
je
t o
f w
ate
r.
You
bu
rn
a b
lac
k s
tar
at
th
e h
ear
t o
f t
he
blu
e a
ppl
e w
e c
all
sk
y.
LARK

GEORGE MACBETH

July

Sunning

Old Dog lay in the summer sun
Much too lazy to rise and run.
He flapped an ear
At a buzzing fly;
He winked a half-opened
Sleepy eye;
He scratched himself
On an itching spot;
As he dozed on the porch
When the sun was hot.
He whimpered a bit
From force of habit,
While he lazily dreamed
Of chasing a rabbit.
But Old Dog happily lay in the sun,
Much too lazy to rise and run.

JAMES S. TIPPETT

A dragonfly

When the heat of the summer
Made drowsy the land,
A dragonfly came
And sat on my hand.

With its blue-jointed body,
And wings like spun glass,
It lit on my fingers
As though they were grass.

ELEANOR FARJEON

Pelting bees

By July the bees have built in the samans:
There are honey-hives in the notches of those burly trees there.
Today is Sunday. I go out and pelt them with white stones,
And duck quick under the river-bank, my feet in the cold water
on the white stones.
How they get up in golden arms then and make a noise like breezes!
I hide and watch and again throw white stones with the strength
of my arm!
Nectar-sweet streams from the rich red honeycombs,
The golden bees blaze with fury in the sun.
I laugh and laugh, pelting white stones from the safety
of Easter river.

IAN McDONALD

A hot day at the school

All day long the sun glared
as fiercely as a cross Head Teacher.

Out on the brown, parched field
we trained hard for next week's Sports Day.

Hedges wilted in the heat;
teachers' cars sweltered on the tarmac.

In the distance, a grenade of thunder
exploded across the glass sky.

WES MAGEE

A rite of summer

Here at the Nagaoka Tenjin Junior High School
some of the girls are washing schoolroom windows,
boys are weeding and sweeping the vast, dusty playground.

But the children there down below my apartment
are busy cleaning out the swimming-pool.
I watch them from my balcony, five storeys up.

After the long winter, the evil-looking, dark green water
with its sinister sediments and vegetable stinks
has finally been let out, leaving a glorious mess behind.

Some of that rich dirt was plum or apricot blossoms
and snowstorms of windblown cherry petals,
or autumn's maples, crimson-leafed, and ginkgo gold.

But now the barefoot schoolchildren, a whole class of thirty-five,
are scrubbing clean the skyblue tiles, the black guidelines
with brooms and hoses, kitchen scrubbers and plastic pails.

Much of the tapwater is playfully splashed on brown-limbed boys
and laughing girls in blue trunks and white t-shirts
till they are soaked to the skin — a kind of annual rite

before the long summer races down those six deep lanes,
now dry, that soon will fill with divers' cries
of joy, and glittering reflections of a cloudless sky.

JAMES KIRKUP

Swimming pool

Splash!   Echo!
Dive!   Echo!
Shout!   Echo!
Dive . . .
Dive into the pool . . .
     The pool . . . the pool.
      Under the pool . . .
     Under the cool . . .
     Under the cool, dolphin pool,
     Under the pool . . .

Splash!   Echo!
Dive!   Echo!
Shout!   Echo!
Dive . . .
Dive into the pool . . .
     The pool . . . the pool.
      Silent and cool . . .
     Under the pool . . .
     Silent and cool, dolphin cool,
     Under the pool . . .

MARIAN LINES

Bed in summer

In winter I get up at night
And dress by bright electric light.
In summer, quite the other way,
I have to go to bed by day.

I have to go to bed and see
The birds still hopping on the tree.
Or hear the grown-up people's feet
Still going past me in the street.

And does it not seem hard to you,
When all the sky is clear and blue,
And I should like so much to play,
To have to go to bed by day?

ROBERT LOUIS STEVENSON

The night sky

All day long
      The sun shines bright.
The moon and stars
      Come out by night.
From twilight time
      They line the skies
And watch the world
      With quiet eyes.

ANON.

School's out

Girls scream
Boys shout
Dogs bark
School's out.

W. H. DAVIES

Holiday

Ding-dong! Ding-dong!
  All the bells are ringing,
Ding-dong! Ding-dong!
  It's a holiday.

Ding-dong! Ding-dong!
  All the birds are singing,
Ding-dong! Ding-dong!
  Let's go out and play!

ANON.

August

August afternoon

Where shall we go?
　　What shall we play?
What shall we do
　　On a hot summer day?

We'll sit in the swing.
　　Go low. Go high.
And drink lemonade
　　Till the glass is dry.

One straw for you,
　　One straw for me,
In the cool green shade
　　Of the walnut tree.

MARION EDEY

Seaside song

It was a
sunboiled brightlight friedegg hotskin suntanned
sizzler of a day

It was a
popsong dingdong candyfloss dodgemcar spaceinvader beachwader
smashing seaside town

We had a
swelltime a welltime a realpellmelltime
a finetime a rhymetime a superdoubledimetime

We beachswam ate ham gobbledup a chicken leg
climbed trees chased bees
got stuck in mud up to our knees
played chase flew in space
beat a seagull in a skating race
rowed boats quenched throats
spent a load of £5 notes
sang songs hummed tunes
played hide-and-seek in sandy dunes
did all these things, too much by far,
that we fell asleep going back by car . . .
from Folkestone.

JOHN RICE

Up on the Downs

Up on the Downs,
Up on the Downs,
A skylark flutters
And the fox barks shrill,
Brown rabbit scutters
And the hawk hangs still,
Up on the Downs,
Up on the Downs,
With butterflies
jigging
like
costumed
clowns.

Here in the Hills,
Here in the Hills,
The long grass flashes
And the sky seems vast,
Rock lizard dashes
And a crow flies past,
Here in the Hills,
Here in the Hills,
With bumble bees
buzzing
like
high-speed
drills.

High on the Heath,
High on the Heath,
The slow-worm slithers
And the trees are few,
Field-mouse dithers
And the speedwell's blue,
High on the Heath,
High on the Heath,
Where grasshoppers
    chirp
      in the
        grass
          beneath.

WES MAGEE

Slowly

Slowly the tide creeps up the sand,
Slowly the shadows cross the land.
Slowly the cart-horse pulls his mile,
Slowly the old man mounts the stile.

Slowly the hands move round the clock,
Slowly the dew dries on the dock.
Slow is the snail — but slowest of all
The green moss spreads on the old brick wall.

JAMES REEVES

Sunbather

the sea yawns

a train rumbles over

the bridge

it rattles the girders for the children
who scramble to wave spades and cornets
they dive under the earthquake of the arch
to feel the thunder to see
the sweating stones shake overhead

and then

and then

the black capped guard

in the distance

waving goodbye

with a red handkerchief

ALAN PERRY

Beachcomber

Monday I found a boot —
Rust and salt leather.
I gave it back to the sea, to dance in.

Tuesday a spar of timber worth thirty bob.
Next winter
It will be a chair, a coffin, a bed.

Wednesday a half can of Swedish spirits.
I tilted my head.
The shore was cold with mermaids and angels.

Thursday I got nothing, seaweed,
A whale bone,
Wet feet and a loud cough.

Friday I held a seaman's skull,
Sand spilling from it
The way time is told on kirkyard stones.

Saturday a barrel of sodden oranges.
A Spanish ship
Was wrecked last month at The Kame.

Sunday, for fear of the elders,
I sit on my bottom.
What's heaven? A sea chest with a thousand gold coins.

GEORGE MACKAY BROWN

Every cloud has a silver lining

Building building building
Castles in the sky
Just lying back and watching
White cloud worlds sailing by.

Dreaming dreaming dreaming
Of a magic place
Where time is unimportant
And you lose all sense of space.

Wishing wishing wishing
I could lose myself inside
Those misty swirling mountains
Where great adventures hide.

Floating floating floating
In a realm of fantasy
Where knights and dragons battle
To set fair maidens free.

Knowing knowing knowing
That tomorrow always comes
Yet imagination flings you
Far out beyond the sun.

ADRIAN RUMBLE

August weather

Dead heat and windless air,
 And silence over all;
Never a leaf astir,
 But the ripe apples fall;
Plums are purple-red,
 Pears amber and brown;
Thud! in the garden-bed
 Ripe apples fall down.

Air like a cider-press
 With the bruised apples' scent;
Low whistles express
 Some sleepy bird's content;
Still world and windless sky,
 A mist of heat over all;
Peace like a lullaby,
 And the ripe apples fall.

KATHARINE TYNAN

Hollingbury

Above the earth fort
        a skylark   singing
            twittering

The stillness as
        the mists roll in
            from the sea

so clear

        the air

here

      the sun

          catching

the line of hills

        in the distance

LEE HARWOOD

September

September

There are twelve months throughout the year,
From January to December —
And the primest month of all the twelve
Is the merry month of September!
Then apples so red
Hang overhead,
And nuts ripe-brown
Come showering down
In the bountiful days of September!

There are flowers enough in the summer-time,
More flowers than I can remember —
But none with the purple, gold, and red
That dye the flowers of September!
The gorgeous flowers of September!
And the sun looks through
A clearer blue,
And the moon at night
Sheds a clearer light
On the beautiful flowers of September!

MARY HOWITT

Apple jingle,
Japple angle

Pickem Packem
Stickem Stackem
Apples in a box

Bitem Munchem
Lickem Crunchem
A Pippin and a Cox

JOHN RICE

Blackberries

Wind roaring loud!
Sky a black cloud,
With fear of thunder!
Weather not heeding,
I run, scratched and bleeding,
Back home with my plunder.

And though Mother's holding
My hand and scolding,
How can I listen? —
So ripe and sweet they are,
Where in their glassy jar
They blackly glisten.

JOHN WALSH

Diary of a church mouse

Here among long-discarded cassocks,
Damp stools, and half-split open hassocks,
Here where the Vicar never looks
I nibble through old service books.
Lean and alone I spend my days
Behind this Church of England baize.
I share my dark forgotten room
With two oil-lamps and half a broom.
The cleaner never bothers me,
So here I eat my frugal tea.
My bread is sawdust mixed with straw;
My jam is polish for the floor.

Christmas and Easter may be feasts
For congregations and for priests,
And so may Whitsun. All the same,
They do not fill my meagre frame.
For me the only feast at all
Is Autumn's Harvest Festival,
When I can satisfy my want
With ears of corn around the font.
I climb the eagle's brazen head
To burrow through a loaf of bread.
I scramble up the pulpit stair
And gnaw the marrows hanging there.

It is enjoyable to taste
These items ere they go to waste,
But how annoying when one finds
That other mice with pagan minds
Come into church my food to share
Who have no proper business there.

Two field mice who have no desire
To be baptized, invade the choir.
A large and most unfriendly rat
Comes in to see what we are at.
He says he thinks there is no God
And yet he comes . . . it's rather odd.
This year he stole a sheaf of wheat
(It screened our special preacher's seat),
And prosperous mice from fields away
Came in to hear the organ play,
And under cover of its notes
Ate through the altar's sheaf of oats.
A Low Church mouse, who thinks that I
Am too papistical, and High,
Yet somehow doesn't think it wrong
To munch through Harvest Evensong,
While I, who starve the whole year through,
Must share my food with rodents who
Except at this time of the year
Not once inside the church appear.

Within the human world I know
Such going-ons could not be so,
For human beings only do
What their religion tells them to.
They read the Bible every day
And always, night and morning, pray,
And just like me, the good church mouse,
Worship each week in God's own house.

But all the same it's strange to me
How very full the church can be
With people I don't see at all
Except at Harvest Festival.

JOHN BETJEMAN

87

This is just to say

I have eaten
the plums
that were in
the icebox

and which
you were probably
saving
for breakfast

Forgive me
they were delicious
so sweet
and so cold

WILLIAM CARLOS WILLIAMS

Signs

Summer's nearly over,
Fields are turning gold,
Every blade of barley
Gives back a hundredfold.

The world is falling silent,
Seems to be on fire,
Swallows now are gathering
All along the wire.

Garden flowers and wild ones,
Nearly half in rags,
Leaves are changing colour,
A hundred different flags.

Sun has done his duty,
And the wild geese fly
In their flapping squadrons
Across the autumn sky.

LEONARD CLARK

Something told the wild geese

Something told the wild geese
    It was time to go.
Though the fields lay golden
    Something whispered — 'Snow'.
Leaves were green and stirring,
    Berries, lustre-glossed,
But beneath warm feathers
    Something cautioned — 'Frost'.

All the sagging orchards
    Steamed with amber spice,
But each wild breast stiffened
    At remembered ice.
Something told the wild geese
    It was time to fly —
Summer sun was on their wings,
    Winter in their cry.

RACHEL FIELD

Season of sport

The pheasant glows and gleams
In his finest autumn plumes.

He is a moving feast of flame,
And yesterday the cornfields curtained him.

He walked through secretly, invisible,
Now he stalks tall, stilted in the stubble.

Any minute now, guns will bark and snap,
And hounds will trigger themselves to grip.

You will pass a scuffed disarray of chaff,
A scrabble of feathers, bloodstained stiff.

GEOFFREY SUMMERFIELD

Autumn

Autumn is the rich season,
the year's tycoon;
great armfuls of
the trees' lost
bullion;
cascades of newly minted
gold;
the season's banknotes —
crinkled, crisp, already
spent.

ADRIAN RUMBLE

Falling leaves

The leaves in autumn
Swing on the boughs
Pushed by the wind,
Backwards and forwards
Far above the ground.
The wind blows hard
And the leaves let go
Their hold,
Flying over the wood
Like a flock of birds
And brown as sparrows
Flying above the house.
The wind lets them fall
Helter skelter
Towards the ground
Or sets them spinning
On a roundabout;
You can watch them
And try to catch them
Coming down.
They crowd together
By walls at corners
Or chase each other
Up the road.
Sometimes when you open
The kitchen door
A leaf blows in
And lies exhausted
On the floor.

STANLEY COOK

October

Autumn in Regent's Park

The footballers
dance in the mist;
it muffles their shouts;
in muted colours
they rise
through the mist
through the trees.

GERDA MAYER

Days that the wind takes over

Days that the wind takes over
Blowing through the gardens
Blowing birds out of the street trees
Blowing cats around corners
Blowing my hair out
Blowing my heart apart
Blowing high in my head
Like the sea sound caught in a shell.
One child put her thin arms around the wind
And they went off together.
Later the wind came back
Alone.

KARLA KUSKIN

Who has seen the wind?

Who has seen the wind?
    Neither I nor you;
But when the leaves hang trembling
    The wind is passing through.

Who has seen the wind?
    Neither you nor I;
But when the trees bow down their heads
    The wind is passing by.

CHRISTINA ROSSETTI

Autumn

A touch of cold in the Autumn night —
I walked abroad,
And saw the ruddy moon lean over a hedge
Like a red-faced farmer.
I did not stop to speak, but nodded,
And round about were the wistful stars
With white faces like town children.

T. E. HULME

October dawn

October is marigold, and yet
A glass half full of wine left out

To the dark heaven all night, by dawn
Has dreamed a premonition

Of ice across its eye as if
The ice-age had begun its heave.

The lawn overtrodden and strewn
From the night before, and the whistling green

Shrubbery are doomed. Ice
Has got its spearhead into place.

First a skin, delicately here
Restraining a ripple from the air,

Soon plate and rivet on pond and brook;
Then tons of chain and massive lock

To hold rivers. Then, sound by sight
Will Mammoth and Sabre-toothed celebrate

Reunion while a fist of cold
Squeezes the fire at the core of the world,

Squeezes the fire at the core of the heart,
And now it is about to start.

TED HUGHES

Aberdeen train

Rubbing a glistening circle
on the steamed-up window I framed
a pheasant in a field of mist.
The sun was a great red thing somewhere low,
struggling with the milky scene. In the furrows
a piece of glass winked into life,
hypnotized the silly dandy; we
hooted past him with his head cocked,
contemplating a bottle-end.
And this was the last of October,
a Chinese moment in the Mearns.

EDWIN MORGAN

The witch's brew

Hubble bubble at the double
cooking pot stir up some trouble.

Into my pot
there now must go
leg of lamb
and green frog's toe,

Old men's socks
and dirty jeans,
a rotten egg
and cold baked beans.

Hubble bubble at the double
cooking pot stir up some trouble.

One dead fly
and a wild wasp's sting,
the eye of a sheep
and the heart of a king;

A stolen jewel
and mouldy salt,
and for good flavour
a jar of malt.

Hubble bubble at the double
cooking pot stir up some trouble.

Wing of bird
and head of mouse.
Screams and howls
from that haunted house.

And don't forget
the pint of blood,
or the sardine tin,
or the clod of mud.

Hubble bubble at the double
cooking pot stir up some trouble!

WES MAGEE

A Hallowe'en pumpkin

They chose me from my brother: 'That's the
Nicest one,' they said,
And they carved me out a face and put a
Candle in my head;

And they set me on the doorstep. Oh, the
Night was dark and wild;
But when they lit the candle, then I
Smiled!

DOROTHY ALDIS

The Witch! The Witch!

The Witch! The Witch! don't let her get you!
Or your Aunt wouldn't know you the next time she met you!

ELEANOR FARJEON

Hallowe'en

This is the night when witches fly
On their whizzing broomsticks through the wintry sky;
Steering up the pathway where the stars are strewn,
They stretch skinny fingers to the waking moon.

This is the night when old wives tell
Strange and creepy stories, tales of charm and spell;
Peering at the pictures flaming in the fire
They wait for whispers from a ghostly choir.

This is the night when angels go
In and out the houses, winging over the snow;
Clearing out the demons from the countryside
They make it new and ready for Christmastide.

LEONARD CLARK

November

November 3rd

A rocket with its stick
jammed into the ground
snatched from the box
when no one was looking

into the garden under my coat
rammed in the earth
when all the backs were turned

Ignition
firing into mud
Stuck fast

Just a couple of sparklers
Mark's Dad had said
as a treat before Guy Fawkes

Now spluttering with rage
    speechless moment then
louder and louder — bellowing

his fury at us
rising higher and higher
'Spoiling everything Everything
Just never enough Never satisfied'

His words like whipping twigs
that sting hot tears
too much shame to hear him
on and on

of how we would have had
some hot tomato soup
and all been happy

not now No
You two put an end to that
now everyone must do without

Because of us
no treats
no happiness

through all the tears
a blackened twisted wreck
of burned-out wood and paper
crushed beneath my boot

MICK GOWAR

Remember, remember

Please to remember
The fifth of November,
Gunpowder, treason and plot;
I see no reason
Why gunpowder treason
Should ever be forgot.

ANON.

Fireworks

They rise like sudden fiery flowers
That burst upon the night,
Then fall to earth in burning showers
Of crimson, blue and white.

Like buds too wonderful to name,
Each miracle unfolds,
And catherine-wheels begin to flame
Like whirling marigolds.

Rockets and roman-candles make
An orchard of the sky,
When magic trees their petals shake
Upon each gazing eye.

JAMES REEVES

Reading a bonfire, top to bottom

Sparks expire just as they meet the stars.
Smoke thins out, dissolved in air.
Fingers of smoke in sparkling gloves reach up.
Smoke as thick as wrists wrestles into darkness.
Tips of flame singe late wandering insects.
Great fists of fire punch bales of smoke into the sky.
Guy's hat has tilted and burns like hair.
The face is a bubbling horror-mask.
Buttons are popping off like fireworks.
He wears a coat of flame and ruin.
The rest of him has sunk into the furnace.
Here the heart's so hot, to look would burn your eyes.
Chestnuts and baked potatoes sweat and crack.
Already ash is piling up like white-hot snow.
The grass that grew here will be slow to come again.
Tomorrow all we'll know is a patch of scorched earth.

GEOFFREY SUMMERFIELD

Anne and the fieldmouse

We found a mouse in the chalk quarry today
In a circle of stones and empty oil drums
By the fag end of a fire. There had been
A picnic there: he must have been after the crumbs.

Jane saw him first, a flicker of brown fur
In and out of the charred wood and chalk-white.
I saw him last, but not till we'd turned up
Every stone and surprised him into flight.

Though not far — little zigzags spurts from stone
To stone. Once, as he lurked in his hiding-place,
I saw his beady eyes uplifted to mine.
I'd never seen such terror in so small a face.

I watched, amazed and guilty. Beside us suddenly
A heavy pheasant whirred up from the ground,
Scaring us all; and, before we knew it, the mouse
Had broken cover, skimming away without a sound,

Melting into the nettles. We didn't go
Till I'd chalked in capitals on a rusty can:
THERE'S A MOUSE IN THOSE NETTLES. LEAVE
HIM ALONE. NOVEMBER 15TH. ANNE.

IAN SERRAILLIER

Fog in November

Fog in November, trees have no heads,
Streams only sound, walls suddenly stop
Half-way up hills, the ghost of a man spreads
Dung on dead fields for next year's crop.
I cannot see my hand before my face,
My body does not seem to be my own,
The world becomes a far-off, foreign place,
People are strangers, houses silent, unknown.

LEONARD CLARK

Posting letters

There are no lamps in our village,
And when the owl-and-bat black night
Creeps up low fields
And sidles along the manor walls
I walk quickly.

It is winter;
The letters patter from my hand
Into the tin box in the cottage wall;
The gate taps behind me,
And the road in the sliver of moonlight
Gleams greasily
Where the tractors have stood.

I have to go under the spread fingers of the trees
Under the dark windows of the old man's house,
Where the panes in peeling frames
Flash like spectacles
As I tip-toe.
But there is no sound of him in his one room
In the Queen-Anne shell,
Behind the shutters.

I run past the gates,
Their iron feet gaitered with grass,
Into the church porch,
Perhaps for sanctuary,
Standing, hand on the cold door ring,
While above
The tongue-tip of the clock
Clops
Against the hard palate of the tower.

The door groans as I push
And
Dare myself to dash
Along the flagstones to the great brass bird,
To put one shrinking hand
Upon the gritty lid
Of Black Tom's tomb.

Don't tempt whatever spirits stir
In this damp corner,
But
Race down the aisle,
Blunder past font,
Fumble the door,
Leap steps,
Clang iron gate,
And patter through the short-cut muddy lane.

Oh, what a pumping of breath
And choking throat
For three letters.
And now there are the cattle
Stirring in the straw
So close
I can hear their soft muzzling and coughs;
And there are the bungalows,
And the steel-blue miming of the little screen;
And the familiar rattle of the latch,
And our own knocker
Clicking like an old friend;
And
I am home.

GREGORY HARRISON

Thunder and lightning

Blood punches through every vein
As lightning strips the windowpane.

Under its flashing whip, a white
Village leaps to light.

On tubs of thunder, fists of rain
Slog it out of sight again.

Blood punches the heart with fright
As rain belts the village night.

JAMES KIRKUP

Giants upstairs

The stormy sky turns black as night
And the forked lightning flashes
As if a giant who needed a light
Was striking enormous matches.

From the clouds comes the sound of thunder
As if we had giants upstairs
Who were moving monster furniture
And knocking over tables and chairs.

In the rain above the town
It thunders louder than before
Like a giant falling down
And rolling over and over along the floor.

STANLEY COOK

No!

No sun — no moon!
No morn — no noon —
No dawn — no dusk — no proper time of day —
  No sky — no earthly view —
  No distance looking blue —
No road — no street — no 't'other side the way —
  No end of any Row —
  No indications where the Crescents go —
  No top of any steeple —
No recognitions of familiar people —
  No courtesies for showing 'em —
  No knowing 'em! —
No travelling at all — no locomotion,
No inkling of the way — no notion —
  'No go' — by land or ocean —
  No mail — no post —
No news from any foreign coast —
No Park — no Ring — no afternoon gentility —
  No company — no nobility —
No warmth, no cheerfulness, no healthful ease,
  No comfortable feel in any member —
No shade, no shine, no butterflies, no bees,
  No fruits, no flowers, no leaves, no birds —
    November!

THOMAS HOOD

December

Winter is here

Clouds sag.
Puddles are glass.
Naked elms — cities of the rook — forsaken.
Red hips where the wild rose flushed.
Cow parsley dried brown.
A few seeds not shed.
Oo! it's cold.
My breath walks before me.
My fingers feel fat.
Snow. Yes, it really is snow at last
Dizzying down like woolly moths
Without a sound.
I want to make a noise.
I want to call everyone out.
I want to shout, 'Look, winter is here!'

OLIVE DOVE

It's winter, it's winter

It's winter, it's winter, it's wonderful winter,
When everyone lounges around in the sun!

It's winter, it's winter, it's wonderful winter,
When everyone's brown like a steak overdone!

It's winter, it's winter, it's wonderful winter,
It's swimming and surfing and hunting for conkers!

It's winter, it's winter, it's wonderful winter,
And I am completely and utterly bonkers!

KIT WRIGHT

Winter

On Winter mornings in the playground
The boys stand huddled,
Their cold hands doubled
Into trouser pockets.
The air hangs frozen
About the buildings
And the cold is an ache in the blood
And a pain on the tender skin
Beneath finger nails.
The odd shouts
Sound off like struck iron
And the sun
Balances white
Above the boundary wall.
I fumble my bus ticket
Between numb fingers
Into a fag,
Take a drag
And blow white smoke
Into the December air.

GARETH OWEN

The snowman

Mother, while you were at the shops
and I was snoozing in my chair
I heard a tap at the window
saw a snowman standing there

He looked so cold and miserable
I almost could have cried
so I put the kettle on
and invited him inside

I made him a cup of cocoa
to warm the cockles of his nose
then he snuggled in front of the fire
for a cosy little doze

He lay there warm and smiling
softly counting sheep
I eavesdropped for a little while
then I too fell asleep

Seems he awoke and tiptoed out
exactly when I'm not too sure
it's a wonder you didn't see him
as you came in through the door

(oh, and by the way,
the kitten's made a puddle on the floor)

ROGER McGOUGH

Snow and snow

Snow is sometimes a she, a soft one.
   Her kiss on your cheek, her finger on your sleeve
In early December, on a warm evening,
   And you turn to meet her, saying, 'It's snowing!'
      But it is not. And nobody's there.
      Empty and calm is the air.

Sometimes the snow is a he, a sly one.
   Weakly he signs the dry stone with a damp spot.
Waifish he floats and touches the pond and is not.
   Treacherous-beggarly he falters, and taps at the window.
      A little longer he clings to the grass-blade tip
      Getting his grip.

Then how she leans, how furry foxwrap she nestles
   The sky with her warm, and the earth with her softness.
How her lit crowding fairytales sink through the space-silence
   To build her palace, till it twinkles in starlight —
      Too frail for a foot
      Or a crumb of soot.

Then how his muffled armies move in all night
   And we wake and every road is blockaded
Every hill taken and every farm occupied
   And the white glare of his tents is on the ceiling.
      And all that dull blue day and on into the gloaming
      We have to watch more coming.

Then everything in the rubbish-heaped world
   Is a bridesmaid at her miracle.
Dunghills and crumbly dark old barns are bowed in the chapel of her sparkle,
   The gruesome boggy cellars of the wood
      Are a wedding of lace
      Now taking place.

TED HUGHES

Stopping by woods on a snowy evening

Whose woods these are I think I know.
His house is in the village though;
He will not see me stopping here
To watch his woods fill up with snow.

My little horse must think it queer
To stop without a farmhouse near
Between the woods and frozen lake
The darkest evening of the year.

He gives his harness bells a shake
To ask if there is some mistake.
The only other sound's the sweep
Of easy wind and downy flake.

The woods are lovely, dark and deep,
But I have promises to keep,
And miles to go before I sleep,
And miles to go before I sleep.

ROBERT FROST

Christmas bells

Five bells all and all bells sing
Gloria Gloria to the King.

Four bells, north, south, east and west,
Ponder an uninvited guest.

Three bells, father, son and spirit
Strike up the bargain we inherit.

Two bells argue, tenor and bass,
Is this the time? Is this the place?

One bell, dumb in its tower of stone,
Alone, alone, alone, alone.

JOHN MOLE

Carolling around the estate

The six of us met at Alan's house
    and Jane brought a carol sheet
that she'd got free from the butcher's shop
    when she bought the Sunday meat.

Jeremy had a new lantern light
    made by his Uncle Ted,
and Jim had 'borrowed' his Dad's new torch
    which flashed white, green and red.

Our first call was at Stew Foster's place
    where we sang 'Three Kings' real well.
But his mother couldn't stand the row
    and she really gave us hell!

We drifted on from door to door
    singing carols by lantern light;
Jane's lips were purple with the cold;
    my fingers were turning white.

Around nine we reached the chippy shop
    where we ordered pies and peas,
and with hot grease running down our hands
    we started to defreeze.

I reached home tired out, but my Mum said,
    'your cousin Anne's been here.
She's carolling tomorrow night
    and I said you'd go, my dear.'

WES MAGEE

Ring out, wild bells

Ring out, wild bells, to the wild sky,
    The flying cloud, the frosty light:
    The year is dying in the night;
Ring out, wild bells, and let him die.

Ring out the old, ring in the new,
    Ring, happy bells, across the snow:
    The year is going, let him go;
Ring out the false, ring in the true.

ALFRED, LORD TENNYSON

Blue wish

When the gas-fire glows
    It tingles with a
        Low
        Blue light.
        It

Dances with a slow
    Flicker of wishing:
Wish I may,
    Wish I might

Have a blue wish
    Always burning,
Noon,
    Burning,
        Night.

KIT WRIGHT

Index of poets

Index of first lines

Acknowledgements

For permission to reproduce copyright material the Editor is indebted to:

The authors for: 'Three days into March', 'shower' and 'Calendar of cloud' by Moria Andrew; 'In the garden in winter' from *Come Along: Poems for Younger Children*, 1978, 'Falling leaves', 'Bluebells' and 'Giants upstairs' from *Come Along Again: More Poems for Younger Children*, 1982, by Stanley Cook; 'Winter is here' by Olive Dove; 'New Year morning' and 'Posting letters' by Gregory Harrison; 'Hollingbury' from *Boston-Brighton* (Oasis Books 1979) by Lee Harwood; 'The nest' from *Here We Go* by Jean Kenward; 'Firefox', 'A rite of summer' and 'Thunder and lightning' from *The Prodigal Son* by James Kirkup; 'May' from *The Agricultural Engineer* (Priapus Press) by John Loveday; LARK by George MacBeth from *Poemcards* (ed. D. and E. Grugeon, Harrap); 'Pelting bees' by Ian MacDonald from *Poetry Introduction 3* (Faber & Faber); 'January moon' by Gerda Mayer; 'First snow' and 'Christmas bells' by John Mole; 'Springburst' from *There's Motion Everywhere* (Houghton Mifflin Company) by John Travers Moore © 1970; 'Aberdeen train' by Edwin Morgan from *Poems of Thirty Years* (Carcanet 1982); 'Winter days' and 'Winter' from *Salford Road* (Kestrel Books 1979) by Gareth Owen; 'Every cloud has a silver lining' and 'Autumn' by Adrian Rumble; 'Anne and the fieldmouse' by Ian Serraillier © 1963 from *Happily Ever After* (Oxford University Press); 'Robin' by Iain Crichton Smith from *A Scottish Poetry Book* (Oxford University Press 1983); 'Giant Winter' by Derek Stuart; 'Now the sleeping creatures waken' by Raymond Wilson.

Aten Press for 'First day of spring' and 'Apple jingle' from *Rockets and Quasars* and 'Seaside song' from *Zoomballoomballistic* by John Rice; Jonathan Cape Ltd and the Executors of the W. H. Davies Estate for 'School's out' from *The Complete Poems of W. H. Davies* and the Estate of Robert Frost for 'Stopping by woods on a snowy evening' from *The Poetry of Robert Frost* ed by E. Connery Lathem; Chatto & Windus Ltd for 'Winter birds' by Leslie Norris from *Mountains, Polecats and Pheasants*; Collins Publishers for 'November 3rd' by Mick Gowar © 1981 from *Swings and Roundabouts*; Christopher Davies Publishers for 'Sunbather' by Alan Perry from *Live Wires*; Andre Deutsch Ltd for 'After breakfast' from *Seen Grandpa Lately?* by Roy Fuller, 'From the winter wind' from *Mind Your own Business* by Michael Rosen, 'Season of sport' and 'Reading a bonfire' from *Welcome and Other Poems* by Geoffrey Summerfield; Dobson Books for 'Hallowe'en' from *Good Company*, 'Fog in November' from *Four Seasons* and 'Earthworm' from *Collected Poems and Verses for Children* by Leonard Clark; Dolphin Concert Productions for 'The vegetable garden and the runaway horse' by Pam Ayres; Faber & Faber Ltd for 'The river in March', 'Swifts', 'Snow and snow' from *Season Songs* and 'October dawn' from *The Hawk in the Rain* by Ted Hughes, 'The trees' and 'Cut grass' from *High Windows* by Philip Larkin; Fontana Paperbacks for 'Blue wish', 'It's winter' and 'The frozen man' from *Rabbiting On* by Kit Wright; Harper & Row Publishers, Inc. for 'Days that the wind takes over' from *Near the Window Tree* by Karla Kuskin © 1975; Harrap Ltd for 'Father and I in the woods' and 'Summer shower' from *Mr Bidery's Spidery Garden* by David McCord; William Heinemann Ltd for 'Things to remember' and 'Slowly' from *The Wandering Moon* by James Reeves and 'Sunning' by James Tippett from *Crickety Cricket!*; Heinemann Educational Books for 'Autumn' by T. E. Hulme from *The Poet's World*; David Higham Associates for 'A dragon fly' and 'The witch! The witch!' by Eleanor Farjeon from *Silver Sand and Snow* (Michael Joseph), 'My mother saw a dancing bear' by Charles Causley from *Figgie Hobbin* (Macmillan) and an extract from *Under Milk Wood* (Dent) by Dylan Thomas; Hodder & Stoughton Children's Books for 'Signs' by Leonard Clark from *The Singing Time*; The Hogarth Press for 'Beachcomber' by George Mackay Brown from *Fishermen with Ploughs*; Macmillan Publishers for 'Weathers' by Thomas Hardy; Macmillan Publishing Company Inc. for 'Something told the wild geese' from *Poems by Rachel Field*; Spike Milligan Productions Ltd for 'Rain' from *Silly Verse for Kids* by Spike Milligan; John Murray Publishers for 'Diary of a church mouse' from

Acknowledgements

Collected Poems by John Betjeman; Oxford University Press for 'May poem' (First published in *Expression*, No.7, 1967) and 'Autumn in Regent's Park' (one section from complete poem entitled 'Three autumns in Regent's Park') by Gerda Mayer © 1984 from *The Candy-floss Tree*, 'In March' by Anne Stevenson © 1974 from *Travelling Behind Glass*; Penguin Books Ltd for 'It's spring' by Kit Wright © 1981 from *Hot Dog and Other Poems* (Kestrel Books); A. D. Peters & Co. Ltd for 'Snow and ice poems' and 'The snowman' from *Sky in the pie* (Kestrel Books) by Roger McGough; Laurence Pollinger Ltd for 'This is just to say' by William Carlos Williams from *The Collected Earlier Poems* (New Directions Publishing Corporation); The James Reeves Estate for 'Fireworks' by James Reeves © 1952; Charles Scribner's Sons for 'August afternoon' from *Open the Door*; Rhymes for Children by Marion Edney © under the Berne Convention; The Society of Authors as the literary representative of the Estate of A. E. Housman for 'Loveliest of trees' from *Collected Poems* Jonathan Cape Ltd) by A. E. Housman; Western Publishing Company Inc. for 'A skiing song for January' by Michael Lewis from *Golden Treasury of Poetry* © 1959.